EXTREME WEATHER

EARTHQUAKES

by Anastasia Suen

AMICUS | AMICUS INK

rubble

cracks

Look for these words and pictures as you read.

machine

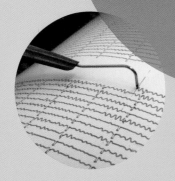

fault line

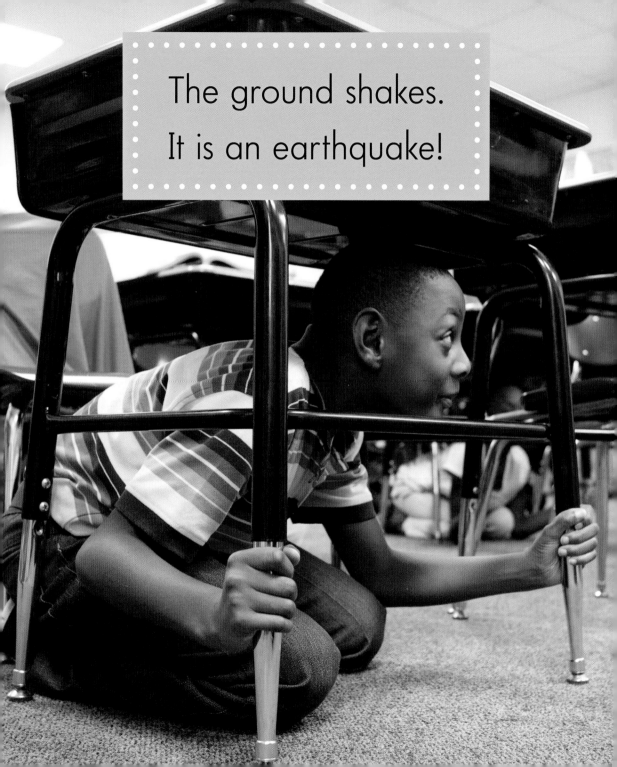

The ground shakes.
It is an earthquake!

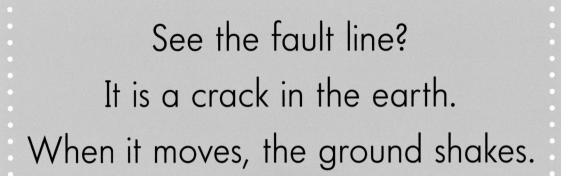

See the fault line?
It is a crack in the earth.
When it moves, the ground shakes.

fault line

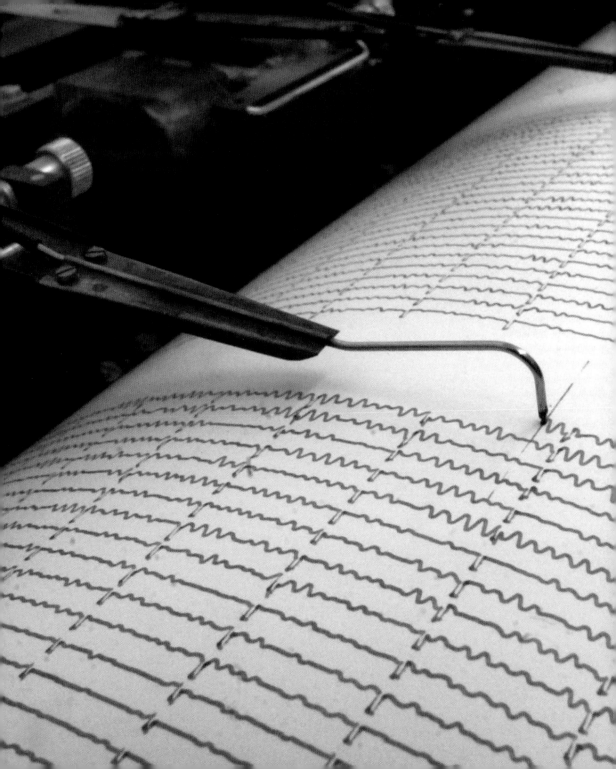

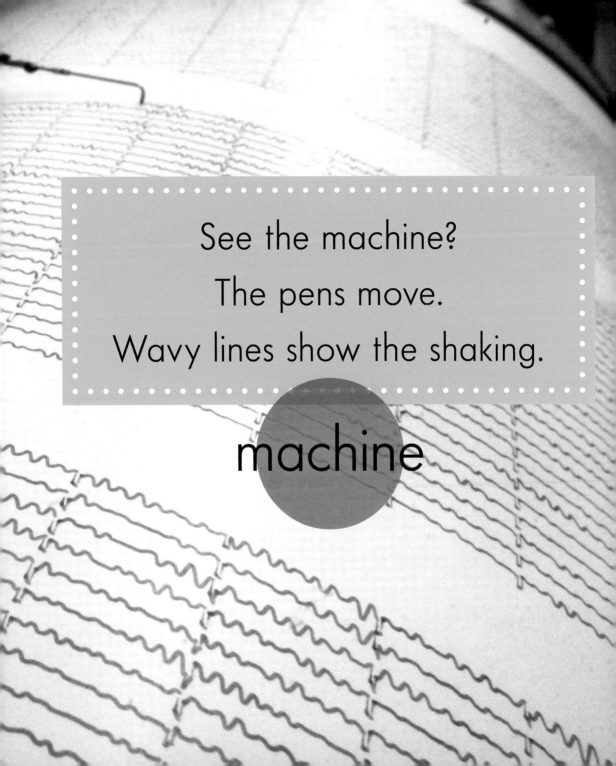

See the machine?
The pens move.
Wavy lines show the shaking.

machine

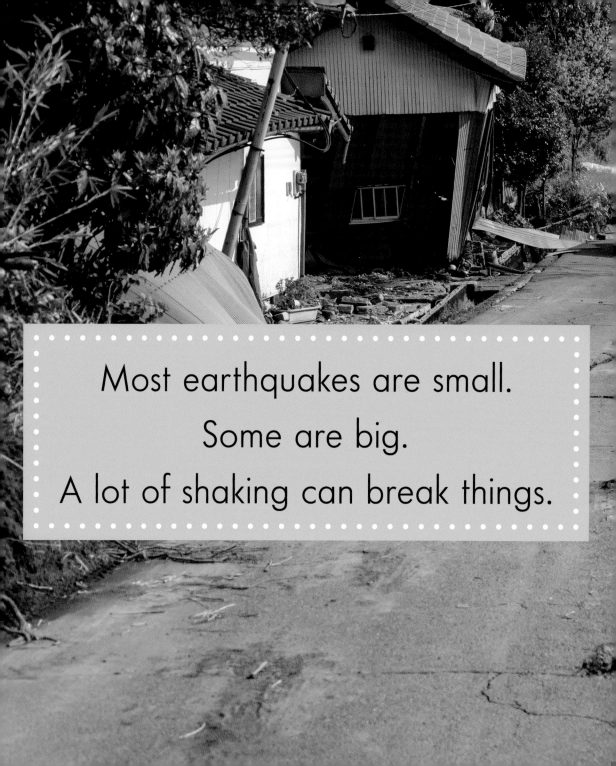

Most earthquakes are small.

Some are big.

A lot of shaking can break things.

cracks

See the cracks?

The wall broke when it shook.

It is not safe.

See the rubble?
The house shook too much.
It fell down.

rubble

Workers help people.
They clean up.

See the rubble?
The house shook too much.
It fell down.

rubble

cracks

See the cracks?
The wall broke when it shook.
It is not safe.

rubble

cracks

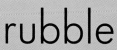

Did you find?

machine

fault line

See the machine?
The pens move.
Wavy lines show the shaking.

machine

See the fault line?
It is a crack in the earth.
When it moves, the ground shakes.

fault line

Spot is published by Amicus and Amicus Ink
P.O. Box 1329, Mankato, MN 56002
www.amicuspublishing.us

Library of Congress Cataloging-in-Publication Data
Names: Suen, Anastasia, author.
Title: Earthquakes / Anastasia Suen.
Description: Mankato, MN : Amicus, [2021]. | Series: Spot.
  Extreme weather | Audience: Ages 4–7. | Audience:
  Grades K–1.
Identifiers: LCCN 2019036320 (print) | LCCN 2019036321
  (ebook) | ISBN 9781681519425 (library binding) | ISBN
  9781681525891 (paperback) | ISBN 9781645490272 (pdf)
Subjects: LCSH: Earthquakes—Juvenile literature.
Classification: LCC QE521.3 .S84 2021 (print) | LCC
  QE521.3 (ebook) | DDC 551.22--dc23
LC record available at https://lccn.loc.gov/2019036320
LC ebook record available at https://lccn.loc.gov/2019036321

Printed in the United States of America

HC 10 9 8 7 6 5 4 3 2 1
PB 10 9 8 7 6 5 4 3 2 1

Alissa Thielges, editor
Deb Miner, series designer
Ciara Beitlich, book designer
Aubrey Harper, photo researcher

Photos by Shutterstock/Nigel Spiers cover,
16; Alamy/Nabaraj Regmi 1; AP/John
Paul Henry 3; Shutterstock/melissamn 4–5;
AP/Jan-Peter Kasper 6–7; Shutterstock/
amata90 8–9; iStock/Paolo74s 10–11;
iStock/Björn Forenius 12–13; iStock/
Konstantin_Novakovic 14–15